Dad had a little box.

It was a present for Mum.

Dad had an idea.

He wanted to make Mum laugh.

Mum and Dad had a party.

Mum gave Dad a present.

Dad gave Mum a big box.

Mum had a smaller box.

"What is it?" she asked.

The present got smaller…

…and smaller

…and smaller.

"This is for you," said Dad.

"And this is for you," said Mum.

"Oh Dad!" said Mum.
"Oh Mum!" said Dad.